"*The Book of Doing* isn't just a book. It's a solution. It's a fountain of youth. It's a reminder that true happiness isn't something you chase. It's something you unlock within yourself."

—Brad Meltzer, bestselling author of *Heroes for My Son*

"In this day of unemployment and economic unrest, where it seems that antidepressants have become a panacea, *The Book of Doing* is a natural pick-me-up from the minute you open it."

—Jill Drossman, clinical psychologist

The Book of Doing
EVERYDAY ACTIVITIES TO UNLOCK YOUR CREATIVITY AND JOY

Allison Arden

Illustrations by Adam James Turnbull

A Perigee Book

A PERIGEE BOOK
Published by the Penguin Group
Penguin Group (USA) Inc.
375 Hudson Street, New York, New York 10014, USA

Penguin Group (Canada), 90 Eglinton Avenue East, Suite 700, Toronto, Ontario M4P 2Y3,
Canada (a division of Pearson Penguin Canada Inc.)
Penguin Books Ltd., 80 Strand, London WC2R 0RL, England
Penguin Group Ireland, 25 St. Stephen's Green, Dublin 2, Ireland
(a division of Penguin Books Ltd.)
Penguin Group (Australia), 250 Camberwell Road, Camberwell, Victoria 3124, Australia
(a division of Pearson Australia Group Pty. Ltd.)
Penguin Books India Pvt. Ltd., 11 Community Centre, Panchsheel Park, New Delhi—
110 017, India
Penguin Group (NZ), 67 Apollo Drive, Rosedale, Auckland 0632, New Zealand
(a division of Pearson New Zealand Ltd.)
Penguin Books (South Africa) (Pty.) Ltd., 24 Sturdee Avenue, Rosebank, Johannesburg
2196, South Africa
Penguin Books Ltd., Registered Offices: 80 Strand, London WC2R 0RL, England

While the author has made every effort to provide accurate Internet addresses at the
time of publication, neither the publisher nor the author assumes any responsibility
for errors or for changes that occur after publication. Further, the publisher does not
have any control over and does not assume any responsibility for author or third-party
websites or their content.

THE BOOK OF DOING

First edition: April 2012
Perigee trade paperback ISBN: 978-0-399-53734-9

PRINTED IN THE UNITED STATES OF AMERICA

10 9 8 7 6

Most Perigee books are available at special quantity discounts for bulk purchases for
sales promotions, premiums, fund-raising, or educational use. Special books, or book
excerpts, can also be created to fit specific needs. For details, write: Special Markets,
Penguin Group (USA) Inc., 375 Hudson Street, New York, New York 10014.

For Scott, Max, and Maya

Dear Reader,

Welcome to *The Book of Doing*. I am excited you have discovered it! To understand what the book is about it will help to understand a bit about how it came to be.

    The Book of Doing is not a book I set out to write. (To be clear, I don't consider this a book I wrote, as much as a book I "made," but I hadn't intended to do that either. I'll explain that, too.) I'm not a writer per se—simply someone who decided one day that I was going to begin moving toward happiness, and truly "living" my life rather than just going through the motions. This book is one of the many happy outcomes of that decision.

    I had attempted to do this once before—the move toward happiness bit—but I got sidetracked, as we often do, by life events. Here's what happened: I was about to leave my job of ten years at the publication *Advertising Age.* I didn't have another job in hand, but I did have the simple notion that I was going to explore my creativity. I always wanted to start my own company, and I had an idea of what I could do, but I didn't think I could truly do it while I was working full-time and raising my children. My husband and I knew it would be difficult to make ends meet if I quit my job, but we decided we were going to make it work. However, just as I was about to step off and begin the exploration, I was offered a promotion and stayed. Within seven months of that promotion, I received another promotion, and there I was—running the show.

    Great, right? In many ways, yes—absolutely—and I realize now how blessed I am for this turn of events. But in other ways, no. I found myself living a very full life and juggling many balls, but often feeling like I was running too fast and going through the motions without any meaningful end. And that didn't feel like living—at all. My friends and I often joked that we were "living the dream," but we didn't think we'd be this harried in the dream.

    I'm not sure what gave me my ultimate moment of clarity: approaching my fortieth birthday, the fact that my thirties had been a total blur, my children suddenly turning ages that I remembered being, or the realization that I had achieved the vision that I set out for myself when I graduated from college. Or perhaps it was meeting a lot of new people as part of my new job, and finding that some of them seemed to be doing a better job of "living"—they seemed happier, freer, and definitely more comfortable in their skin. Many of them had less responsibility than me and were possibly a bit older, but did that matter? Whatever the cause, I knew something had to change.

I began to wonder if I needed to leave my job to find my passion, or to wait to find it until I was through with this busy part of my life. Or could I just commit myself to figuring it out, while keeping my day job and all the responsibility that comes with being a full-time, working, married mom?

I decided to try to figure it out. A few months into this decision, life happened again. The economy collapsed, and my professional life and personal life were filled with people and companies trying to reinvent themselves, become more open to change, and understand what made them tick. As the publisher of the leading media brand for the advertising industry, *Advertising Age*, I was engaged in an industry in which creativity has been largely limited to one department called the Creative Department. But in this new world order, there were calls for everyone to be creative. Creativity could no longer be isolated to a single department; it needed to be set free.

I had always considered myself creative, but not artistic, and I tended to access my creative side only for little side projects when I had the time. Now I found myself without much time, and in a professional environment where the economy and marketplace were forcing businesses everywhere to reinvent themselves. Our reinvention would require a creative approach—an ability to consider everything we were doing with an open mind, a fresh perspective, and an enthusiastic energy when life around us seemed pretty dark. Because of the industry I was in and the position I held within it, I probably spent more time than most thinking about the subject of creativity—wondering where it came from, and how I could ignite it in myself and my team.

I kept coming back to my childhood.

Growing up, I had always been an arts-and-crafts kid. I loved coloring and painting, playing with clay, and making lanyard bracelets with my friends. But as I became older, I gave up the crayons and glitter for more "important," "serious," grown-up activities, like "real" schoolwork and hanging out with friends, then later building a career and a family. I'm not alone in this; author Sir Ken Robinson talks about the creativity crisis and how the education system eliminates the artist within each of us at a very early age.

However, as an adult, when I made the commitment to begin to consciously explore the things that gave me joy, I came to a realization. As I decorated Valentine's Day cupcakes with my daughter, or went to crafts stores to buy supplies for new projects, I found myself exhilarated by the activities and excited about buying and playing with supplies that I hadn't used in the longest time. It reawakened a feeling in me that felt more profound than you would imagine possible from working with ribbon and sequins. Turns out, I still loved arts and crafts as an adult—potentially more than my kids—but there was something more.

I thrived on the sense of exploration, and the activity that comes from making things, testing new concepts, getting my hands dirty, focusing inward, seeing my project taking shape, and, of course, always finishing projects off with a glorious set of googly eyes. What I loved most of all was the physical act of "doing." With it came a simple focus on pure delight.

I thrived on the freedom and energy that came from doing. But was my creativity locked up in the paint and glitter, or could I bring all of what I loved about those activities into my work and personal life?

I decided to approach each of my daily activities with the same sense of joy and wonder I found in my "side projects." On the weekends, with my kids, rather than the usual lunch and park visit, we created new activities—such as self-designed tasting tours, movie making to cheer up a sick friend, and gourd mailings to spread joy and test the boundaries of the postal service. We made them up as we went along, and it brought back the sense of spontaneity and freedom I felt as a child. My children felt the same. Everything around me felt better and brighter.

The same thing happened at work. We began to rethink the business we were in and questioned our own potentially self-imposed boundaries as to what we and our brand were capable of creating. We realized that, as a magazine and a website, we were not about print on paper or pixels on a screen, but about the content we created and the people who were part of it. In our purest form, we were simply in the business of helping people get smarter about advertising, marketing, and media. When viewed through this lens, many new opportunities became clear for a brand that had been in business for eighty years. We rethought how we packaged products, tested new concepts, and engaged with our community in unexpected and exhilarating ways. We became more open to the possibilities and gave more people within the organization a voice in our future and a seat at the table.

During this time, I also began writing again. Writing had been my favorite subject in school, but as I grew up, I never felt like I had anything to write about. In my job, the only writing I did was in emails and proposals. But as I started approaching life as I approached arts and crafts, it dawned on me that I was living a metaphor of sorts. My life was like an arts-and-crafts project—a canvas or piece of clay that was always in process and only as colorful, interesting, and exciting as I made it. The more I put into it, the better it became and the more I learned from it. I woke up one day with words in my head that made me realize that what I had been doing could be formulated into a book that could perhaps help others in the same way it was helping me. I started putting my ideas on paper. Within a few hours I had created a chapter outline, and within a few days I had written enough where chapters began to form. I had never expected to write a book, but I was so excited about what I was creating that I couldn't stop, which led me to my agent and my editor, and, eventually, to this book, which leads me to you.

The Book of Doing asks you to do the things I love to do

most—to make things and engage in the act of doing. My hope is that these exercises will unlock your creativity, joy, and a childlike sense of wonder, much as they did for me.

I haven't been alone in this; others have joined me in this exploration and unlocked their own joy and creativity along the way. To be sure, everyone's journey is different. However, there is one absolute: Nothing happens without doing.

With joy and creativity,

ALLISON

Find *The Book of Doing* online: bookofdoing.com

or

Join the conversation on Twitter: #bookofdoing

INTRODUCTION

Thomas Edison once said, "If we all did *the things* we are capable of doing, we would literally astound ourselves." Unfortunately, though, this isn't the case for most of us.

Instead, we've left behind what we love to do because there is too much to get done.

We've convinced ourselves that what we are currently doing is all we can do.

We've gotten to the point at which we're so good at something, we just tell others to do it, rather than doing it ourselves.

We've left behind the things we loved to do most in childhood as we've built our grown-up lives.

We think our joyful pursuits are too frivolous, we're too busy, we're too old, we're afraid to look silly. Perhaps we don't think we're good enough, and certainly not good enough to make a living at it.

It's time to change this mind-set.

Consider the joy you took from the things you loved to do as a child. When you were called for dinner you couldn't stand to be pulled away from whatever you were doing—crafts, games, playing a sport rather than simply watching one—you were having so much fun. It is that sense of childhood delight and wonder that we need to rediscover. By bringing it forward, we can tap into what makes us feel most present and alive. Seriously. We must play if we are to live!

Go ahead. Roll up your sleeves and get to it. Dig deep, play hard, leave your fears behind, and find the joy in everything you do. Channel your passions—don't abandon them. Should we give something up just because we can't make a living from it? Or can we channel our passion to make what we do for a living that much better? Can we engage in the art of doing?

What is doing? Creating, making, mastering, perfecting, helping, inventing, initiating, experimenting, learning, drawing, changing, constructing, reading, moving, trying, challenging, testing, helping, building, writing, singing, dancing, hosting, cooking, painting, tasting, sharing, smelling, imitating, playing, enjoying, being, giving, acting, celebrating, loving. All joyful pursuits that, as adults, we've turned into chores. We've minimized the value of what these acts of personal creation can fuel in our society: the perspective, centeredness, and sense of accomplishment they give us.

It is time to embrace the art that can live within each of these acts of doing.

It is time to realize that the things you *love* to do are the things you *have* to do, because they feed your soul and help you stay in the moment.

It is time to find ways to turn the things you have to do into the things you love to do because it will make them better.

It is time to do the things that make you happiest.

In the same way we have allowed technology to infiltrate every area of our lives, we must allow our creativity and passions to infuse our daily activities. We must stop compartmentalizing our creativity and our passion and set them free. As you do, you will see how your doing, creativity, and passion can connect you in a real way with others around you.

Through daily acts of doing, you can begin to reawaken your senses and reconnect with yourself, other people, and the beauty in the world around you. By returning to acts of doing—making, playing, exploring—you will test the boundaries of the possible and find the spark within you. Pay attention to the things that make you happiest, allow your mind to be free, and begin getting comfortable sharing your greatest gifts with the world.

Where do you start? This book is chock-full of activities that will jump-start your doing and tap into your creativity. Keep it close as a reference and instruction manual. Use it to introduce new activities into your life spontaneously or as part of a long-term plan. Each of these projects can be done alone, with your friends and family, or shared with others you may not even know—yet. Maybe they will help raise awareness, raise money, or inspire others in a way you may not be able to imagine right now. Or they may simply make you smile.

It is time to recapture the joy in the mundane. It is time to rediscover the remarkable. It is time to embrace your greatest passion and joy every day. No need to vacate your life. You will find all you need in your daily acts of doing.

THE LAWS OF DOING

1. **Everything starts with nothing.** Sometimes it takes a few steps for you to begin to see your creation. Keep going.

2. **It is never too late to start doing.** Age can be an excuse regardless of how old you are. Don't let it stand in your way—ever.

3. **Disengage from your device.** Mobile devices and social media are amazing creations that add value in many ways, but we must disconnect and focus on doing in order to be present for the people and the world around us. Shut it off, hide it in a drawer, whatever you need to do. It will all still be there when you get back.

4. **You can always find the time for the things you want to do.** If you look closely enough, it is possible to find time to do the things you really want to do. Even if you cannot spend as much time as you would like doing exactly what you want, every minute you spend is worthwhile and helps you plant seeds for the future.

5. **Choose doing.** If you have a choice between doing nothing and doing something, do something.

6. **Turn what you have to do into what you love to do.** If you approach a project or a job as a chore, it will be one. Reevaulate why you're doing what you're doing. If there is a reason for why you have to do it, find the joy in your actions.

7. **Don't be distracted by the red bouncing ball.** There will always be something with the ability to pull your attention away. Figure out what it is, and learn how to overcome it. Decide what is important and commit your time to it.

8. **Learn from doing.** Nobody starts out an expert, and often the biggest lessons are learned from failure. If what you've done doesn't come out how you hoped, learn from that. Don't look at it as a waste of time. You learned from the act of doing. Carry your lessons forward to your next project.

9. **Set a vision, but be open to the exploration.** Many of your best experiences will come from the exploration. You may end up with an unexpected and exhilarating outcome. Approach each project with a sense of wonder.

10. **Getting started is the first step.** If you have a vision but don't know exactly how to get it done, take the first step. The first step may be finding someone who can help. Future steps will become clear through your initial exploration. If your project doesn't have a mandatory outcome, set a vision for what you'd like to accomplish so you have a place to start and an idea of where you're heading. But be open to the discovery (see number 9!).

11. **Taking a break can make your project better.** Sometimes you need to step away from a project to be able to see it with new eyes and a fresh perspective.

12. **The things worth doing aren't easy.** The things worth doing often come with some fear and frustration. Don't be scared away. It is the challenging parts that can make the end result sweeter.

13. **The things worth doing take time.** Technology has turned us into an instant gratification culture. Sometimes things take longer than you expect. Unless there is some pending deadline, there is no need to rush a project just to get to the end.

14. **Do for you.** Taking time to do something for yourself is not selfish. It makes you and everything around you better.

15. **Do and tell.** If you're excited about what you're doing, don't be shy. Tell your friends. They'll encourage you when you hit frustration points and help keep you going.

16. **Don't worry about what others think about what you're doing, and don't worry about what others are doing.** Worrying about someone else's project or spending energy wondering what they think about yours is a sure way to hamper your creativity. Let it flow freely without negativity, apprehension, or self-consciousness. Some of the most amazing things have been accomplished by people others thought were crazy.

17. **Let your creativity bring out the creativity in someone else.** Don't allow someone to say they're not creative. Creativity exists within each of us. Use your creativity to help inspire creativity in others around you. Pay it forward.

18. **Finish your projects.** Always commit yourself to finishing your project from the outset. A genuine commitment creates a genuine result.

Get a good idea and stay with it. Dog it,
and work at it until it's done and done right.

—Walt Disney

NOW ON TO SOME ACTIVITIES TO GET YOU STARTED!

THE MOST CREATIVE PEOPLE IN THE WORLD SAY THEY TAKE THEIR INSPIRATION FROM THE WORLD AROUND THEM. ENGAGING IN DAILY ACTS OF DOING ENABLES YOU TO PARTICIPATE IN LIFE IN A MORE MEANINGFUL WAY SO EVERYTHING YOU DO BECOMES A SOURCE OF INSPIRATION FOR YOU.

I'VE ADDED LOTS OF PERSONAL ANECDOTES TO SHARE HOW THESE ACTIVITIES HAVE HELPED ME GAIN PERSPECTIVE, SLOW DOWN, FIND MY PURPOSE, AND HAVE MORE FUN. I HAVE ALSO ADDED SOME STORIES OF OTHERS THAT HAVE INSPIRED ME ALONG THE WAY.

EVERYONE'S EXPLORATION IS DIFFERENT. USE THESE TO GUIDE YOU, BUT ADD YOUR OWN IDEAS TO MAKE IT WORK FOR YOU. PLEASE SHARE YOUR IDEAS WITH ME AT BOOKOFDOING.COM, AND CHECK OUT SOME PICTURES AND VIDEOS FROM MY ADVENTURES.

CREATE YOUR OWN PERSONAL BEST ICE CREAM SUNDAE

ICE CREAM FLAVORS: _____

_____

SYRUPS: chocolate, butterscotch, caramel, marshmallow, raspberry, hot fudge

TOPPINGS: sprinkles, M&M's, chocolate chips, peanut butter chips, cookie dough

FRUIT: bananas, strawberries, cherries

Give it a name.

cherry fudge choc vanilla, M&M sprinklicious

FUN FACT: The first documented ice cream sundae was created in 1892.

Large dollop
of whip cream

Quintessential
cherry on
top

Chocolate
Chips

Chopped
Nuts

Chocolate
Fudge
Sauce

Real Heavenly

ash

e Cream

CREATE YOUR OWN

13

MASTER HOW TO SAY "HELLO" "PLEASE" AND "THANK YOU" IN FIVE LANGUAGES

PIG LATIN DOES NOT COUNT, BUT SIGN LANGUAGE DOES

Sometimes you can be speaking the same language and still not have clear communication. Speaking in a language that others can understand gives you the chance to connect with so many more different and interesting people. Learn to speak the language of others by mastering these phrases in other languages. While you're at it, consider what may be hindering communication with others who speak your language. Are you using words they understand, or presenting yourself in a way they can relate to?

	HELLO	PLEASE	THANK YOU
MANDARIN	Ni Hao (knee-how)	Qing (ch-ihng)	Xie Xie (shi-e shi-e)
SPANISH	Hola (OH-lah)	Por favor (POHR fah-VOHR)	Gracias (GRAH-syahs)
FRENCH	Bonjour (bone-zhur)	S'il vous plait (SEEL voo PLEH)	Merci (MEHR-see)
HEBREW	Shalom (sha-LOME)	B'evakashah (beh-vah ka-shah)	Toda (toh-DAH)
JAPANESE	Konnichiwa (kon-nee-chee-WAH)	Onegai (oh-neh-gigh)	Domo arigato (doh-moh ah-ree-GAHtoh)

Amharic

NOTE: There are 7 billion people on the planet speaking 7,000 languages, according to National Geographic.

YOU'VE JUST ADDED AT LEAST 15 NEW WORDS TO YOUR VOCABULARY

NOW REMOVE THREE: CAN'T, NEVER, AND STUPID.

Sometimes we're our own worst enemies, holding ourselves back from things we'd enjoy if we'd only try. Removing these three words from your vocabulary, or considering the impact they have on you and others, is a great first step to setting yourself free. Don't let them exit your mouth; don't let them enter your mind.

Are there any other words you want to eliminate?

Do not let what you cannot do
interfere with what you can do.

—Coach John Wooden

THROW A THEMED PARTY

Whether you dress up as pirates for a pirate and wench fest, or go with a time-period party, a themed event mixes up the status quo, inspires creativity, and gives people a reason to act silly, which can serve as a necessary stress reliever.

We visit family on the same weekend each year when their town hosts Pirates and Wenches Weekend. The entire town dresses as pirates for two days and nights and walks around saying, "Aaaargh!" We've become the Pirate Family Aaaarden. It is totally absurd, but brings the whole town together and gets people's creative juices flowing through costume making, pirate-ship-building competitions, and many other swashbuckling activities. Don't like pirates? Pick another genre.

PIRATE PARTY

VIBE: Pirate ship

DECORATIONS: Netting, anchors, and skulls

DRESS: Pirate and wench garb

MENU: Seafood and turkey legs

ACTIVITY: Treasure hunt

FAVORS: Eye patches and rum

FUN FACT: International Talk Like a Pirate Day is September 19.

MARTINI-TASTING PARTY

VIBE: Speakeasy

DRESS: Flapper outfits, feather boas, pinstripe suits, and bowler hats

MUSIC: Big band

SETTING THE MOOD: Period movies and photos from that era

COCKTAILS: Martinis of all kinds

FAVORS: Martini glasses

MY THEMED PARTY

THEME:

VIBE:

DRESS:

MENU:

ACTIVITY:

FAVORS:

Not a costume party person? Follow Sean Combs's lead and set a color theme. My friend Avian had all her guests dress in white for her birthday party just as P. Diddy did. It was fun to see her friends get so excited planning their outfits before the big event, and it made the party especially beautiful. Think white is overdone? Pick a different color.

GO WINDOW SHOPPING

Conventional wisdom is that window shopping gives you ideas on what to buy. Instead, use it as an opportunity to inspire your creativity rather than as a way to inspire you to spend money. A walk down the street or through a mall gives you the chance to admire other people's creativity at play in store windows. Window dressers often create magical displays, not just during the holiday season. I've spied an enormous shoe crafted from clothes hangers, and a purse and necktie created out of many spools of thread. This is a cost-free activity that can help you see new ways to turn everyday items into something amazing.

FIND A WINDOW THAT INSPIRES YOU. DRAW IT HERE.

Life is not a spectator sport.
If you're going to spend your whole life
in the grandstand just watching what goes on,
in my opinion you're wasting your life.

—Jackie Robinson

RECAPTURE A FAVORITE CHILDHOOD ACTIVITY

WHAT WERE YOUR THREE FAVORITES?

_____

_____

_____

DO THEM.

Just like I took up writing again, my husband, Scott, also recaptured a favorite childhood activity. After a twenty-year hiatus, he started playing the drums again. Scott and his friends used to jam in his basement for hours when they were younger. At thirty-seven, he joined a band and became friends with the bass player, who was starting a business. He thought Scott would be a perfect colleague, and this friendship led Scott to a whole new career much better suited to his personality and happiness. Plus he began playing in bars downtown, which was a fun new activity for us and our friends.

LEARN TO CODE

COMPUTERS HAVE A LANGUAGE ALL THEIR OWN, ACTUALLY SEVERAL. IT CAN BE INTIMIDATING IF YOU HAVE NO EXPERIENCE, BUT HERE IS A SIMPLE PLACE TO START. THE FOLLOWING STEPS WILL TEACH YOU TO CODE A WEB PAGE IN HTML:

1. Download a basic text editor (e.g., Notepad for Windows or Text Editor for Mac).
2. Create a folder on your desktop. Name it "My Picture."
3. Find any image (GIF, JPEG, etc.) and place it in your "My Picture" folder.
4. Open a plain text file (in Notepad or Text Edit).
5. You'll need to prepare the basic page structure by placing the following HTML markup in the text document:

```
<html>

<head></head>
<body>

<img src="">

</body>

</html>
```

6. Between the quotation marks of the <img src="\"> tag you'll want to place the name of the image that is in your "My Picture" folder.

So if the image that I had saved had the file name of photo.jpg, it would read as <img src="photo.jpg">.

THE FINAL CODE WOULD LOOK LIKE THIS:

```
<html>

<head></head>
<body>

<img src="photo.jpg">

</body>

</html>
```

7. Now save your text file in the "My Picture" folder with an .html extension. If the file does not have an .html extension, your browser will not know to read it as a web page and it will not render correctly.
8. Open your .html file using the browser of your choice. You should see the image on the web page.

CONGRATULATIONS! You have just developed a basic web page. Want to learn more? You can go to www.w3schools.com, which has plenty of free documentation on learning HTML and CSS and designing web pages.

DRAW YOURSELF AS A CARTOON CHARACTER

GO UP A HILL AND THEN

I did this on my birthday trip to Tuscany. After what felt like a very unsatisfying run, I found a crazily inclined driveway next to my hotel and ran up and down again three times. The freedom of running downhill was so exhilarating that I did it over and over. I ran, but if I was more daring I would have done it on a bicycle. Use whatever mode of transportation makes you happiest.

DOWN REALLY FAST

EAT MORE FIBER

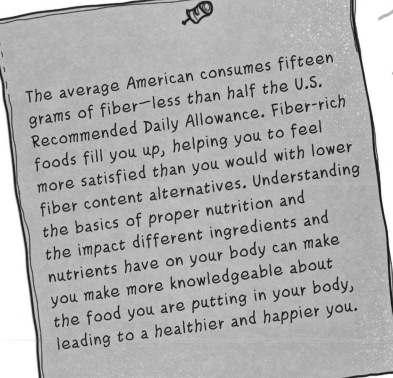

The average American consumes fifteen grams of fiber—less than half the U.S. Recommended Daily Allowance. Fiber-rich foods fill you up, helping you to feel more satisfied than you would with lower fiber content alternatives. Understanding the basics of proper nutrition and the impact different ingredients and nutrients have on your body can make you make more knowledgeable about the food you are putting in your body, leading to a healthier and happier you.

MAIL SOMETHING

DID YOU KNOW?↓

you can send anything *through* the mail (at your own risk) without any packaging? Just include enough *postage* and the address and make sure it can't rot. Send something surprising to a friend or friends. I mailed *pumpkins* to my friends and got a squash in return. This experiment tested the boundaries of an established way of thinking and inspired creativity in someone else .

NO PACKAGING NECESSARY

MAILING YOUR WRAPPER-LESS OBJECT

1. Pick the object you want to mail.
2. Write the address, apply postage stamps, and perhaps add a little message to the recipient.
3. Place in mailbox.
4. Await call from happy recipient.

CONSIDER THIS: If we all did it, we would spread a lot of joy and potentially save the postal service, too. If you're mailing something that really does require wrapping, decorate the box or envelope using markers or stickers. It will make it much more intriguing and exciting for the recipient to open.

The true secret of happiness lies in taking a genuine
interest in all the details of daily life.

—William Morris

FLOSS

It can add years to your life. Amazing, right? I remember the first time someone shared this fact with me. It was at a business lunch, and we were sitting at a table where no one knew each other. The random piece of information served as a great icebreaker and sparked some lively and animated conversation. I was amazed by the little tidbit, and later learned that by removing excess food from your gumline, you are preventing germs and unwanted antibodies from entering your bloodstream. Multiple studies have shown a link between flossing and lower rates of diabetes and heart disease. It also makes your time with the dental hygienist a lot less painful.

Consider what interesting knowledge you can share that might create an opportunity to connect with people around you and help them learn something important.

SKETCH A PICTURE OF SOMEONE OR SOMETHING YOU SEE EVERY DAY

SIT STILL FOR LONGER THAN YOU HAVE IN A WHILE, AND SEE SOMETHING FROM A NEW PERSPECTIVE.

TRAIN TO PARTICIPATE

IN A

SOMETHING - A - THON

MARATHON, BIKE-A-THON, BOWL-A-THON. GIVE YOURSELF ENOUGH TIME TO PRACTICE SO YOU CAN DO IT WITH EASE.

Never run before? Start with ten minutes and build yourself up by five minutes each time you go. I couldn't run a mile until I turned thirty and had my son. Then I realized it might be the only way I got to exercise in my new role as Mom. Not long after, some work friends and I decided to run a marathon. I've since run two full marathons and countless half marathons. It's an incredible way to raise money for a good cause, and gets me doing something I never thought I could. Running has also taught me wonderful lessons about achieving your personal best. When I was done with my first marathon, I truly believed I could do anything, and I got a lot of exercise along the way!

BE INSPIRED BY A DISH YOU LOVED IN A RESTAURANT AND ADD YOUR OWN SPIN

I had a wonderful orange salad at Union Square Café in New York City. I had never had a salad before where the primary ingredient was a fruit. It was so fresh and surprising. They also used the Cara Cara orange, which was a beautiful pink shade. For my own version I added a navel orange as well to create a color contrast with the pink of the Cara Cara. I also substituted Manchego cheese because I didn't have the ricotta salata. It was delicious!

Orange Salad for two

- 1 Cara Cara orange
- 1 navel orange (I like the combination of colors)
- Olive oil
- Salt
- Manchego cheese (you can use ricotta salata, too)
- Pignoli nuts

Peel oranges and cut each widthwise into six pieces. Arrange on small plates. Squeeze rinds into a ramekin, preserving juice for dressing. Add a drop of olive oil and a dash of salt. Beat until blended. Drizzle over oranges. Shave cheese slices on top of oranges. Sprinkle with pignoli nuts and serve.

IMITATE A COCKTAIL...

I once had a spicy vodka drink in a Mexican restaurant. It was fruity and tropical yet spicy, which made it so interesting and unexpected. I tweaked the recipe a bit to cut down the sweetness. If you like it with a bit more kick, use more vodka and less rum.

DIABLO EN EL BIQUINI

1 ounce spiced vodka

1 ounce pineapple juice

1 ounce passion fruit juice (passion fruit puree can be made into juice)

1 ounce Malibu rum

FUN FACT: Milk and pineapple juice are the only liquids that soften spice.

... OR A MOCKTAIL

I had this at a spa once when we took my mom to celebrate her birthday.
The champagne glass made it feel celebratory without the added alcohol.

SPARKLING PEAR BELLINI

Fill champagne glasses
3/4 of the way with
pear cider.

Add 1/8 glass of
peach nectar.

Fill the remainder
with orange juice.

Mix and enjoy.

CREATE STATIONERY WITH YOUR INSIGNIA TO WRITE LETTERS OR THANK-YOU NOTES.

In the marketing industry there is a lot of discussion about building a personal brand, which is a way of expressing what you stand for. Just like a product, your personal brand represents what the world can expect from you on a consistent basis. For this exercise, think about what your logo might be if you were a product. What would it look like? Would someone you know think that it represented you over anyone else?

HOW TO: Once you've designed your insignia, scan it into a computer and save the file as a JPEG. From here you can insert it into a document to print as stationery, print on a transfer sheet to iron onto clothing, or print on sticker paper to use on just about anything! All these supplies are available in an office-supply store or craft shop.

Life isn't about finding yourself;
it's about creating yourself.

—George Bernard Shaw

MAKE YOUR HOLIDAY GIFTS THIS YEAR

Recruit a few friends to make gifts with you. Each person decides what they want to make. Buy the supplies and then arrange a hideaway together for a weekend to make them. These will be gifts people will treasure and you will have a lot of laughs in the process. My friend Nancy has been doing this with her childhood friends for years. What a wonderful tradition! I've given you a few pages to figure out who you'll make gifts for, to sketch a few ideas, and to create your supplies list.

GIFT RECIPIENTS

_____

_____

_____

_____

_____

GIFT IDEAS

_____

_____

_____

_____

_____

SUPPLIES

_____ _____ _____

_____ _____ _____

_____ _____ _____

_____ _____ _____

_____ _____ _____

SKETCH YOUR IDEAS HERE.

PICKLE SOMETHING

My friends Jackie and Angela and I took a pickling class at the Brooklyn Kitchen before Angela's wedding. Angela had decided she wanted to make jars of pickled string beans to give as her wedding favors, along with a Bloody Mary recipe.

As the wedding day drew near it became clear that Angela was not going to get around to the project, so Jackie and I took it on—all 116 jars. We recorded video of the whole activity (hilarious) and thankfully didn't give anyone botulism. I strongly recommend starting with a smaller test batch, but really—it was a ton of fun and a gesture of kindness that made us all happy.

PICKLED STRING BEANS

Our own creation, which we perfected during our 116-jar adventure.

> 2 1/2 pounds fresh string beans
>
> 2 1/2 cups distilled white vinegar
>
> 2 cups water
>
> 1/4 cup salt
>
> 1/2 pound garlic cloves, peeled
>
> 1 bunch fresh dill weed
>
> 1 pound small spicy red peppers
>
> 3/4 teaspoon red pepper flakes (optional)

Sterilize 6 (half-pint) jars with rings and lids and keep hot. Cut string beans to 1/4 inch shorter than your jars.

In a large saucepan, stir together the vinegar, water, and salt. Bring to a boil over high heat. In each jar, place 1 garlic clove, 1 sprig of dill, 2 red peppers, and 1/8 teaspoon of red pepper flakes. Pack string beans into the jars so they are standing on their ends.

Ladle the boiling brine into the jars, filling to within 1/4 inch of the tops. Wipe top rim of the jar so no moisture gets captured under the lid. Seal the jars with lids and rings. Place in a hot water bath so the jars are covered by 1 inch of water. Simmer but do not boil (approximately 180 degrees) for 10 minutes to process. Remove from the pot. Cool to room temperature. Test jars for a good seal by pressing on the center of the lid. It should not move. When jars are cooled you should hear a "pop" to signal the lids are sealed. Refrigerate any jars that do not seal properly. Let pickles ferment for 2 to 3 weeks before eating.

HELP SOMEONE

As my pickling story demonstrates, helping comes in all shapes and sizes. Whether you volunteer in a soup kitchen, help a child with their homework, or make a donation to a charity or someone in need, there are lots of opportunities to do something good for someone else and find fulfillment in the process.

BUILD SOMETHING OUT OF NATURAL MATERIAL

A SNOWMAN, A SAND CASTLE, A TOTEM POLE MADE OF ACORNS, OR A REPLICA OF A BUILDING MADE OUT OF STICKS. NO NEED TO BUY SUPPLIES; USE THE ONES YOU ALREADY HAVE AND THE NATURAL MATERIALS YOU HAVE AROUND YOU. TAKE A PICTURE OF WHAT YOU MADE. ATTACH THE PHOTO HERE.

My favorite natural display is the Holiday Train Show at the New York Botanical Garden. An artist has created 140 miniature replicas of New York City landmarks ranging from Yankee Stadium to the Statue of Liberty. The entire display is built with leaves, tree sap, fruits, bark, and all other natural materials. It brings delight to thousands of visitors each year.

GO FOR A WALK IN THE RAIN

My children and I went outside on a crazy rainy day to go see a *puppet* show in Central Park. My son was not that enthusiastic about the idea, but we wound up having so much fun splashing in the puddles on the way home and seeing more worms than you'd ever imagine existed in New York City. My kids still talk about it!

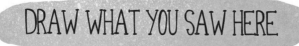

DRAW WHAT YOU SAW HERE

WATCH MOVIES THAT HAVE WON OR BEEN NOMINATED FOR AN ACADEMY AWARD

Make it an event. Invite friends and provide popcorn or even a meal that suits the movie. Appreciate all the things that make award-winning movies— the storytelling, the music, the costumes—every detail contributes to the experience, and many people's talents went into making it amazing. Take the time to appreciate what they have created.

When my husband and I were dating, we spent a snowy day watching *The Godfather* and *The Godfather: Part II*. Part II is the first sequel ever to win the Oscar, and for good reason. If you decide to watch the Godfather movies, if at all possible, watch them in one afternoon so you can appreciate the mastery with which Francis Ford Coppola weaves together the generations. Try watching them with someone who has seen them before so he or she can help you connect the dots or point out interesting details you might miss during your first viewing. Pair your viewing with spaghetti and meatballs, and some red wine for good measure.

MAKE A MOVIE OF YOUR OWN

My first movie was a birthday gift for my sister on her fortieth birthday. I did a tour of our childhood neighborhood featuring lots of interviews with people wishing her a happy birthday. It was a fun way to recap her first half and kick off what I call Phase Two. I used an old video camera and the iMovie software on my Mac to edit it, overlay music from that period, and roll credits of all who participated. It was fun for me to put together and my sister loved it.

Now it's your turn. If you don't have a video camera, see if a friend has one. Most smartphones now have video capabilities, too. Can't make a video? Create an amazing montage by pulling together pictures that tell a story and make a digital scrapbook.

MY CINEMATOGRAPHIC IDEAS

CONSTRUCT A HAPPINESS BOARD

A HAPPINESS BOARD IS A BULLETIN BOARD THAT YOU HANG IN A PROMINENT LOCATION AND USE TO DISPLAY YOUR FAVORITE PICTURES AND MEMENTOS.

Mine sits on the wall in my office facing my desk, and includes some favorite pictures (my husband on a hammock on our honeymoon, my sister and I holding our daughters after a Father's Day race we ran to raise money for prostate cancer the year our dad had it, one of my mom with my son, and many others of and with good friends.) It also holds cards with images I like, and tickets and menus from events I've enjoyed over the years. It makes me smile and reminds me of what is truly important—special people and special moments.

SHOW WHAT YOU WILL PUT ON YOURS.

LISTEN TO MUSIC YOU ENJOY AND REDISCOVER MUSIC YOU HAVEN'T PLAYED IN A WHILE

Whether it's the music you grew up with or your favorite sound track from a play or movie, try to surround yourself with music as often as you can—while you're driving, putting away groceries, getting dressed to go out.

MY TEN FAVORITE SONGS ARE:

1 _____

2 _____

3 _____

4 _____

5 _____

6 _____

7 _____

8 _____

9 _____

10 _____

There are a ton of digital products to help you explore music you love. Check out Pandora to find music that shares the same DNA as your favorites, and Discovr to visually explore music with similar sounds. These are fun uses of technology to expose you to something new based on the things you already love.

CHANGE SOMETHING "UNMOVABLE"

YOUR BIRTHDAY
A ROOM
YOUR HAIR
YOUR POINT OF VIEW

I relocated my birthday to the Tuesday before Thanksgiving because I realized September had just become too busy with things that I didn't have control over—back to school, budgets, and work-related events. The new day has been so much better for me, as well as providing a fun, spontaneous celebration for my friends on a week that tends to be less hectic for all of us. There is an added sense of mischief as we feel as if we're getting away with something—like fooling the birthday gods!

NOTE: People might look at you a little strangely, but ultimately if something isn't working for you, and it's impacting your happiness, then it simply needs to be changed.

Be yourself; everyone else is already taken.

—Oscar Wilde

MIX UP THE SEATING ARRANGEMENT AT A DINNER PARTY

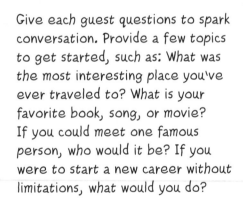

Give each guest questions to spark conversation. Provide a few topics to get started, such as: What was the most interesting place you've ever traveled to? What is your favorite book, song, or movie? If you could meet one famous person, who would it be? If you were to start a new career without limitations, what would you do?

Ideal conversation must be an exchange of thought, and not, as many of those who worry most about their shortcomings believe, an eloquent exhibition of wit or oratory.

—Emily Post

DELIGHT A NEIGHBOR WITH HOMEBAKED COOKIES

RAINBOW COOKIES

This is a cookie I always saw in the store but never knew how they made it. They looked like they would be SO hard. One night, my niece, Stephanie, came over and taught my daughter, Maya, and me how to do it. Mystery solved, and not so hard after all. Just needed to find a good teacher!

Makes 8 dozen cookies

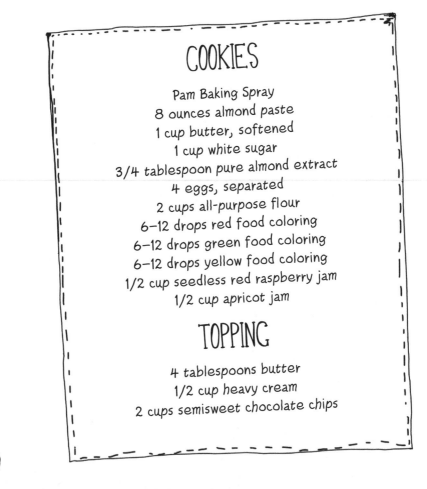

COOKIES

Pam Baking Spray
8 ounces almond paste
1 cup butter, softened
1 cup white sugar
3/4 tablespoon pure almond extract
4 eggs, separated
2 cups all-purpose flour
6–12 drops red food coloring
6–12 drops green food coloring
6–12 drops yellow food coloring
1/2 cup seedless red raspberry jam
1/2 cup apricot jam

TOPPING

4 tablespoons butter
1/2 cup heavy cream
2 cups semisweet chocolate chips

Preheat oven to 350 degrees F. Generously spray three 9x13 cookie sheets with baking spray (contains flour, unlike regular Pam).

In a large bowl, break apart almond paste with a fork or grate paste and cream together with butter, sugar, almond extract, and egg yolks. When mixture is fluffy and smooth, stir in flour to form dough. In a small bowl, beat egg whites until soft peaks form. Fold egg whites into the dough. Divide dough into three equal portions. Mix one portion with red food coloring, one with green food coloring, and one with yellow food coloring. (You want rich colors, as they'll fade during baking.) Spread each portion onto one of the prepared cookie sheets. Dough will be thick and difficult to spread; I suggest using a small knife and small strokes.

Bake 10 to 12 minutes, until lightly browned. Cool for about 10 minutes and then carefully remove from sheet and cool completely on wire racks.

Once cooled, place green layer onto a piece of plastic wrap large enough to wrap all three layers. Spread green layer with raspberry jam, and top with yellow layer. Spread with apricot jam, and top with red layer. Wrap tightly with plastic wrap. Place heavy pans and/or cutting boards on top of wrapped layers to compress. Chill in the refrigerator at least 8 hours, or overnight.

In a saucepan, melt 2 tablespoons butter, 1/4 cup heavy cream, and 1 cup chocolate chips until smooth. Unwrap layers from plastic wrap and top with melted chocolate spread evenly. Refrigerate unwrapped until chocolate is firm (about 1/2 hour to 1 hour). Repeat steps to melt another batch of butter, heavy cream, and chocolate. Remove layers from refrigerator and flip. Cover the other side in chocolate. Refrigerate until firm.

Once chocolate is hardened, run a long, sharp knife under hot water and wipe dry. Slice off the edges of the chocolate-covered layers to make an even rectangle. Reheat the knife often to make the cutting easier. Slice into small, even squares.

WANT TO HOST A COOKIE SWAP? Invite a number of guests. Have each person bring a few dozen of one type of home-baked cookies, plus a container so each guest can go home with a sampler of each. Make sure your guests bring enough so you can have a sampling plate of each selection. A delicious, albeit high-calorie way to spend an evening!

CRAFT SOMETHING SPECIAL OUT OF A SENTIMENTAL ARTICLE OF CLOTHING

IDEAS: A THROW PILLOW, A SATCHEL, A BULLETIN BOARD COVERING

We did this with some of my daughter's T-shirts to create throw pillows for her bed that were uniquely hers. They also had fun messages on them that I liked her to see—"Most Likely to Change the World" and "It's What's on the Inside That Counts" are a few of my favorites. My mother-in-law helped with the sewing and was excited to be part of our project. Now my daughter has a sentimental pillow made with love by her grandma, who also got the job done long before I ever could!

SUPPLIES:

Article of clothing

Needle

Thread

Stuffing

Embellishments: paint, buttons

NEEDLE
AND
THREAD

STUFFING

HOST A COOKBOOK DINNER PARTY

Assign each guest to make a dish from a specific cookbook. Start simple. Go Mexican with Rick Bayless's *Mexican Everyday*—the recipes don't require lots of obscure ingredients so they feel manageable. For Italian food, I'm partial to Arthur Schwartz's *Southern Italian Table*, because his parents lived on my street growing up, and because he learned to enjoy red wine while he cooks from the man I considered my adopted grandfather, "Grandpa B" Caesar Benvenuto. Plus his recipes are delicious!

Do BBQ with my former colleague Lisa Fain, aka the Homesick Texan. Her recipes are simple and infused with a true passion for down-home cooking. If you're more adventurous, take a page from *Julie and Julia*. Assign recipes from *Mastering the Art of French Cooking* by Julia Child, Louisette Bertholle, and Simone Beck. Consider making the meal a party to celebrate Bastille Day!

Doing it is what makes a dream come true.

—Oliver Platt as Elmo's Fairy Godperson, CinderElmo

COMPOSE A LIST ON YOUR BIRTHDAY OF THREE THINGS YOU'D LIKE TO ACCOMPLISH THIS YEAR

USE THE NEXT PAGE TO MAKE YOUR LIST.

Give it to a friend and ask *them* to give it to you in your birthday card next year. Celebrate the ones you've accomplished and don't get down on yourself if you don't get to all of them. Assess what stopped you from getting the others done, and chart out a plan to make it happen in the year ahead.

Note: Birthday just passed? Do it on New Year's instead.

MY _____ YEAR

1 _____
_____
_____
_____

2 _____
_____
_____
_____
_____

3 _____
_____
_____
_____
_____

LEARN TO MAKE SOMEONE ELSE'S SIGNATURE DISH

Spend a day with your mom, dad, aunt, uncle, grandmother, or someone else you love and learn to make their signature dish. One day you'll crave it and want to make it yourself. Now you'll have the recipe and a wonderful memory of a day well spent.

MY NANA'S KNISH RECIPE

1 1/2 cups sifted flour
Salt
1 cup vegetable oil
12 medium russet potatoes, peeled and chunked
3 medium yellow onions, peeled and cut in thin wedges
Ground black pepper
1 egg, beaten with a drop of water

Mix flour and a bit of salt (Nana's recipes weren't exact) in a bowl. Make a well in the center and add 1 cup plus 2 tablespoons warm water and 2 tablespoons oil. Mix to make dough and knead. Divide dough into three pieces. Cover with a clean kitchen towel and let rest for 30 minutes.

Put potatoes into a large pot, cover with cold water, and bring to a boil. Cook until soft, about 30 minutes. Drain, then place in a large bowl. Mash the potatoes. Cover the bottom of a frying pan in oil and cook onions over medium heat, until soft and translucent, stirring all the while. Add onions to potatoes and mash until reasonably smooth. Season to taste with salt and pepper.

Preheat oven to 375 degrees F.

Roll out each pod of dough individually on a floured board to approximately 15 inches in each direction. Brush the dough with egg mixture, then spoon a quarter of the potato mixture onto the dough to form a rectangular shape, approximately 2x12 inches. Wrap the dough over as if to form a jelly loaf. Turn over seam side down and brush with egg mixture again. Repeat with each section of dough.

Bake on a wax paper–lined cookie sheet until lightly brown, approximately 25 minutes. When cooled, cut widthwise in 1-inch pieces and serve, or wrap uncut in tinfoil and freeze until you are ready to heat and serve.

_____'s _____ RECIPE

INGREDIENTS
_____   _____
_____   _____
_____   _____
_____   _____
_____   _____

DIRECTIONS
_____
_____
_____
_____
_____
_____
_____
_____
_____
_____
_____
_____
_____
_____
_____

PERFECT A SIGNATURE DISH AND MAKE IT WHAT YOU'RE KNOWN FOR

I created *the chocolate turkey one year on Thanksgiving: chocolate-covered pretzel rods and twists formed the body and plumage, with dipped dried fruit for the face, wings, and waddle.*

WRITE YOUR OWN RECIPE HERE.

MY SIGNATURE DISH

INGREDIENTS

_____   _____
_____   _____
_____   _____
_____   _____
_____   _____

DIRECTIONS

_____
_____
_____
_____
_____
_____
_____
_____

USE CUPCAKES AS YOUR CANVAS

These tiny morsels of yum give you the opportunity to create miniature, edible masterpieces. Whether for a specific occasion, to test different techniques, or to sample combinations of delicious toppings, decorating cupcakes is a happy exploration in culinary creativity.

FUN ACTIVITY: Set up a cupcake bar next time you serve dessert. A platter of unfrosted cupcakes with a host of different topping options is all you need. Allow your guests to decorate their own. It is fun to watch people carefully assemble their perfect cupcake and delightful to watch as they enjoy eating their creation.

Whatever course you decide upon,
there is always someone
to tell you that you are wrong.
There are always difficulties
arising which tempt you
to believe that your critics are right.
To map out a course of action
and follow it to an end
requires courage.

—Ralph Waldo Emerson

"LEARN TO PLAY A MUSICAL INSTRUMENT

(OR SOMETHING ELSE YOU'VE ALWAYS SAID YOU WOULD DO)

My friend Anne always wanted to play the cello. So one day, when she was in her early fifties, she finally decided to give it a try. She found a teacher, and every Saturday she would take her cello in a case on her back on the New York City subway to her lesson. It took her a year to have "Twinkle, Twinkle, Little Star" sound like it should, but the joy that overcomes her when she tells me about her practicing and playing are enough to make me smile for days. Perhaps you didn't have the discipline as a kid. You do now.

TRANSCRIBE THE WORDS TO A FAVORITE SONG

PICK ONE THAT REMINDS YOU OF SOMEONE SPECIAL IN YOUR LIFE. WRITE THE LYRICS HERE.

Copy this and give it to a friend to let him or her know you're thinking of them.

EXTOL THE VIRTUE OF THE APPLE

Why should you extol the virtues of the apple, you ask? There are more than 500 varieties of apples. One apple contains up to 8 grams of fiber—one-third of your daily allowance and more than any other fruit. Apples protect against Parkinson's and Alzheimer's. That's an amazing piece of fruit.

I'm also quite taken by the avocado. Consider the color, the different textures, and the fact that the pit keeps guacamole from oxidizing. Consider what other incredible things you might be overlooking in your everyday life.

KNOW YOUR APPLES

McIntosh (1 and 4): The inspiration for the name of the Macintosh computer, as it was the favorite fruit of one the Apple employees who worked on the original invention.

Granny Smith (5): Grown in New Zealand, Australia, and the western United States (California and Arizona).

Red Delicious (3): Originally called "Hiatt's Hawkeye" after Jesse Hiatt, the farmer who discovered it.

Golden Delicious (4): Considered one of the most important apples of the twentieth century, especially for breeding other apples.

Jonathan (2): Beautiful red. Good for cooking with meats and making applesauce.

COLOR THEM HERE

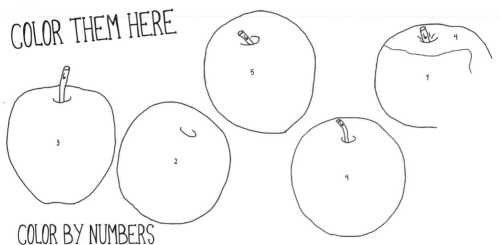

COLOR BY NUMBERS

1 = light red   2 = medium red   3 = dark red   4 = yellow green
5 = light green (Crayola calls this color Granny Smith Apple)

MY GRANDMOTHER'S APPLE CAKE RECIPE

BAKE WITH THEM

5 APPLES

2 EGGS

3/4 CUP SUGAR

INGREDIENTS

1/4 CUP SUGAR MIXED WITH CINNAMON

1 TEASPOON VANILLA

1 CUP FLOUR

1/2 CUP RAISINS

1/2 CUP CHOPPED WALNUTS

INSTRUCTIONS

Peel and cut the apples into eighths and place in an 8x8 greased baking dish. Mix raisins and walnuts together and add to apples. In a large mixing bowl, mix the eggs, sugar, and vanilla. Gradually add the flour until batter is smooth. Pour the batter over the apple, raisin, and walnut mixture. Be sure raisins are covered in batter so they do not burn. Sprinkle sugar and cinnamon mixture over the top.

Bake for 1 hour at 350 degrees F.

Other fun projects to consider for the amazing apple: Make a shrunken apple head doll, cut an apple in half and dip it in paint to create a stamp, or inscribe a message on an apple and mail it to a friend.

Curiosity about life in all of its aspects, I think, is still *the secret of great creative people.*

—Leo Burnett, advertising executive credited with creating Tony the Tiger, the Jolly Green Giant, the Keebler Elves, and many other advertising icons

BECOME CURIOUS

ASK MORE AND DEEPER QUESTIONS.

WHAT DOES IT MEAN?
WHY DOES IT MATTER?
WHO DOES IT IMPACT?

YOU NEVER KNOW WHAT
YOU'LL FIND OUT OR
BEGIN TO UNDERSTAND.

LEARN THE EVOLUTION OF SOMETHING THAT INTERESTS YOU

DRAW IT. HOW WILL IT EVOLVE NEXT?
FROM MUSICAL INSTRUMENTS
TO FASHION TO THE TELEPHONE,
THE WORLD IS ALWAYS CHANGING.

WHERE DID IT START?

HOW DID IT START AND WHY?

WHAT DID IT BECOME?

WHAT CHANGED?

WHAT SHOULD IT BE NEXT?

WHY?

BECOMING A PERSON WHO CAN ANTICIPATE CHANGE IS A SKILL
THAT CAN HELP YOU BETTER PREPARE FOR WHAT LIES AHEAD.

INVENT A NEW TRADITION

My invented tradition: Bloodies at the Gate. My friend Jackie and I created this to get us over the blues of Sunday business travel. Now whenever we have to go away, we meet at the airport and have a Bloody Mary before our flight. It's a tradition we cherish and it has made many a flight delay much more fun. Happily, the tradition has spread to others who now send us pictures of themselves enjoying their preflight Bloody when we can't be with them!

ADOPT A HOLIDAY THAT YOU'VE NEVER CELEBRATED

It's an opportunity to learn something about another culture and try some new foods, songs, and expressions. Plus it gives you another reason to celebrate! Some good ones to try are Chinese New Year, Purim, Cinco de Mayo, Bastille Day, and Oktoberfest.

Attach a photo from the celebration

WAKE UP
EARLY AND
GO OUTSIDE TO
WATCH THE SUNRISE

REUSE A CONTAINER
FOR ANOTHER PURPOSE

Decorate it with something that makes you smile. As a kid I made a piggy bank out of a bleach container. You can still do that, but there are lots of other things to make, too, like bird feeders, vases, and pencil holders. And today the containers are much prettier to start!

You have to color outside the lines once in a while if you want to make your life a masterpiece.

—Albert Einstein

READ THE BIOGRAPHY OF SOMEONE WHOSE WORK AND LIFE HAVE ALWAYS INSPIRED YOU

SOME GREAT ONES INCLUDE:

Einstein: His Life and Universe by Walter Isaacson

The Last Lion: Winston Spencer Churchill by William Manchester

I Know Why the Caged Bird Sings by Maya Angelou

John Adams by David McCullough

Eleanor Roosevelt, volumes 1 and 2, by Blanche Wiesen Cook

At the suggestion of my friend Lori, I limited my reading one year to only biographies. I learned so much in that year and was awakened to how much you can learn from the experiences of others. You'll likely be surprised by the challenges people had to overcome to get to the place where they became world famous.

PLANT A HERB GARDEN

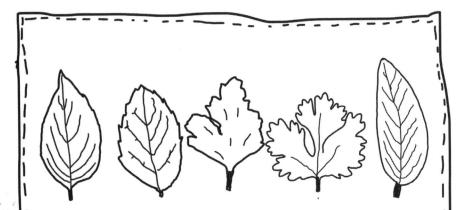

You don't need a big garden to grow your own—just a pot, some soil, herb plants or seeds, water, and sunlight. Fresh herbs are so much better tasting than the dried variety, they smell delicious, and they're easy to grow.

MAKE POPSICLE STICK HERB MARKERS

Color these labels, then laminate them and attach them to Popsicle sticks to mark your herb garden.

BASIL

MINT

PARSLEY

CILANTRO

SAGE

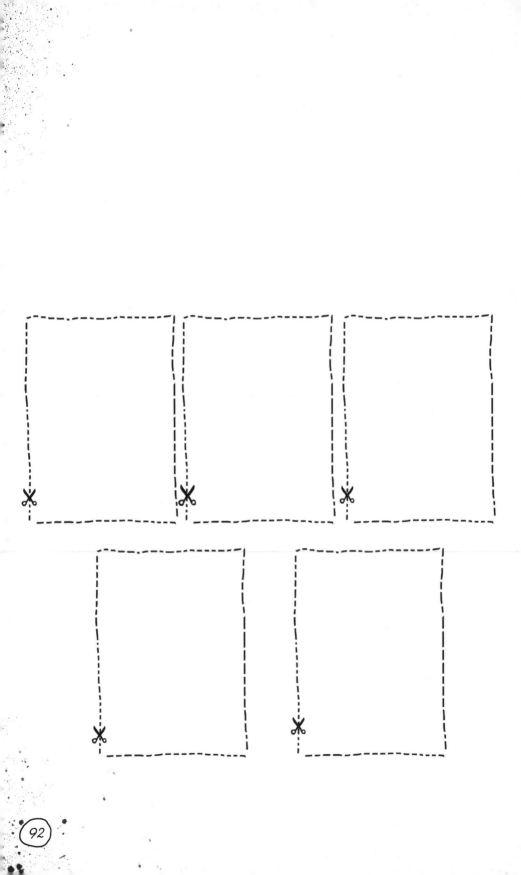

92

MAKE SOMETHING WITH THE HERBS IN YOUR GARDEN

Try basil, tomato, and fresh buffalo mozzarella

or mint, feta, and watermelon.

You can serve them as a salad dressed with a bit of olive oil and some cracked black pepper, or create an hors d'oeuvre by stacking small pieces of each ingredient and skewering them together with a toothpick. Drizzle a bit of olive oil on the platter before serving.

HOST A CREATIVE COMPETITION OR A CREATIVE COLLABORATION

COMPETE

My friend Meilyn and her friends competed for the honor of "Best Burger Maker," and had a ball sampling and perfecting their recipes before the final competition. Your competition doesn't have to involve cooking at all—it can be as simple as "What Can You Do with a Butternut Squash?" as I did with my son's class at Thanksgiving time. They created felt-covered butternut squash turkeys, aliens, and high-fashion models to name a few. It's an opportunity to get people thinking creatively and have fun in the process.

COLLABORATE

The Wertheim sisters—Margaret and Christine—grew up in Queensland, Australia, and were inspired by work they saw by the Institute For Figuring. They combined their knowledge of science and art with their love of crocheting to create coral-like figures that reminded them of the Great Barrier Reef near their hometown. They were so excited by their work that they started a creative collaboration called the Hyperbolic Crochet Coral Reef to raise awareness about the terrible impact rising temperatures and pollution are having on this natural wonder of their homeland. The homage to the reef, which began with the twin sisters at their coffee table crocheting small figures, has attracted volunteer knitters and crocheters all over the world, and the tribute has grown to many thousands of feet long. This creative collaboration combines the sisters' passions all in one incredible and colorful project, and has inspired so many others to get involved.

Your creative collaboration doesn't have to span the globe to have a meaningful impact on you and others.

What will yours be?

COOK OR BAKE WITH AN INGREDIENT YOU'VE NEVER USED BEFORE

IDEAS: YEAST, TRUFFLES, SHORT RIBS, OR SAFFRON

RECIPE

INGREDIENTS

_____   _____
_____   _____
_____   _____
_____   _____
_____   _____

DIRECTIONS

_____
_____
_____
_____
_____
_____
_____
_____
_____
_____
_____
_____
_____
_____

WEAVE A FRIENDSHIP BRACELET FOR YOUR FAVORITE FRIEND AND MAKE YOURSELF A MATCHING ONE

It's amazing how something simple and symbolic can be so meaningful. One of my best friends recently went through a terrible time due to her daughter's illness. Since we couldn't be together while her daughter was going through treatment, we each wore matching bead bracelets to feel connected. Thankfully, her daughter has recovered and is back to a normal teenage life, but these simple bracelets of string and beads were a blessing for us at a very tough time.

Tape string to a piece of cardboard or to the edge of a table—it will be easier for you to master your stitches with the string or lanyard held taut.

COBRA STITCH

1
- Hold two pieces of lanyard, approximately 3 feet long each, side by side.

2
- Fold them in half forming two loops and four strands.

3
- Fold the two loops across the four strands, creating an opening. Pull the two loops through to form a knot.

4
- Separate the strands so one of each color remains in the center, and one of each color falls to each side.

5
- Pick which color will be your lead string and which will be the second string. Form a loop with the lead string and cross over the center strings.

6
- Place the second string over the lead string, pull underneath the center string, and pull through the loop formed by the lead string.

7
- Repeat beginning with the same lead string each time. The color used as the lead string should appear in the center of the stitch.

8
- When you've reached the desired length, slip the strings through the starting loop, tie a knot, and snip the ends.

9
- SUCCESS!

PLAY WITH COLOR

Whether through your clothing choices, furnishings, or accessories, color tells a story and creates a mood. As a New Yorker, I've always tended toward a lot of black in my wardrobe, but a few years ago my friends and I committed ourselves to wearing color on days we were feeling down to brighten our mood and surroundings. It works and projects a happy spirit onto the world.

WHAT DO COLORS SAY?

RED — Warm, confident

ORANGE — Creative, enthusiastic, economical

YELLOW — Happy, sunny

GREEN — Optimistic, natural

BLUE — Calm, stable, trusting

PURPLE — Regal, inspiring

WHITE — Innocent, fresh, pure

BLACK — Powerful, depressed, sophisticated

WRITE YOUR NAME IN BUBBLE LETTERS
AND COLOR IT, OF COURSE!

SPEAK TO SOMEONE YOU'VE KNOWN FOREVER ABOUT SOMETHING YOU'VE NEVER DISCUSSED

Some questions to consider: Tell me a story I've never heard before or a story you've never told anyone. Who you most admire and why? What is your favorite dessert? What was the best thing your parents ever taught you?

RECORD THE ANSWERS HERE.

YOU'LL BE AMAZED HOW MUCH YOU DON'T KNOW ABOUT SOMEONE YOU LOVE.

MAKE A PIGGY BANK

DECORATE AN EMPTY COFFEE CAN,
AND THEN CUT A HOLE IN THE PLASTIC
COVER TO FIT YOUR SPARE CHANGE.

You'll be surprised by what you can buy for yourself,
put away in a savings account,
or make as a donation to charity.

WHAT WILL YOU DO
WITH YOUR LOOSE CHANGE?

EXPERIENCE A CITY OR ACTIVITY THROUGH THE EYES OF A GUIDE

Whether for a town, museum, or Disney World, good guides are well educated and will teach you things you didn't know before or wouldn't have known otherwise. Make a list of places you'd like to explore in the next six months, locally or somewhere farther. Find a way to make it happen.

START A BOOK CLUB

THE FIRST ANNUAL GRAND PRAIRIE RABBIT FESTIVAL
– Ken Wheaton –

Give each member of the club questions about the text and the characters prior to reading. It will make the reading experience and discussion much richer when you're together.

My son's fourth-grade class does this. It helps them gain a much deeper understanding of the material as they read. It's a wonderful practice to bring into adult life, so you can appreciate literature in a deeper way.

eat pray love ELIZABETH GILBERT

Or use *The Book of Doing* for your book club and turn it into a "Doing Club" instead.

WELCOME IN THE SEASONS

WITH EACH NEW BEGINNING, CHANGE SOMETHING IN YOUR HOUSE OR OFFICE TO ACKNOWLEDGE AND APPRECIATE THE SEASON.

My sister-in-law Lori decorates her home with snowmen each winter. She now has 642 of them, each of their own design. The effect is magical, and turns a cold season warm.

EAT OATMEAL FOR BREAKFAST EVERY DAY FOR THREE WEEKS

I started this a few years ago, and it made my winter happier. Here's what I found out—oatmeal helps boost your serotonin levels, which has been discovered to be lacking in people suffering from depression. The serotonin boost you get from oatmeal really can make you happier. Add some chopped apples and walnuts. The apples add some sweetness and the walnuts give you an essential oil that keeps your lips smooth. Pure delight.

PAINT A PICTURE OF A LANDSCAPE

YOUR BACKYARD, A PARK, A SUNSET

SHARE YOUR CREATION WITH OTHERS.

My friend Cammy takes an art class every Tuesday night. Each week she sends me a mobile picture of her latest creation. It is such a sweet ritual, and it always surprises and delights me, and connects me to her even when I can't see her. Sharing her artwork is her way to test her creativity and to get comfortable with putting her work out in the world, one person at a time.

ATTACH A COPY OF YOUR ARTWORK HERE.

TASTE A SLICE OF PIZZA FROM EVERY SHOP IN TOWN

Bring your friends along. Rate each pizza on crust, sauce, cheese, and overall flavor. Pick your favorite. When you're done, set a date to do a food tasting for another favorite.

I did this with my children and some friends. Rather than scarfing down our slices as we would normally do, we slowed down, thanks to the score card, so we could actually take the time to think about the flavor of each part. We've since expanded to other foods. The food tastings are always an adventure and always delicious, plus they've made us more discriminating about our food selections and what we like.

Don't feel like running all over town? Invite your friends over and assign each to bring a sample from a different pizza shop.

PIZZA SCORE CARD

Pizza Shop #1

Taster	Crust	Cheese	Sauce	Overall

Pizza Shop #2

Taster	Crust	Cheese	Sauce	Overall

Pizza Shop #3

Taster	Crust	Cheese	Sauce	Overall

MAKE A POPSICLE STICK REPLICA OF YOUR FIVE FAVORITE PEOPLE

Use crayons, markers, yarn, and cloth to create your wooden tributes. Stick them someplace you'll see them often—in a planter, as a bookmark, as a refrigerator magnet—or give them as gifts to the people who inspired them.

READ THE ORIGINAL VERSION OF YOUR FAVORITE CHILDHOOD STORY

THERE ARE AMAZINGLY POWERFUL MESSAGES IN THE TEXTS THAT MOST LIKELY WENT OVER OUR HEADS WHEN WE WERE CHILDREN.

Suggested reading: *Alice's Adventures in Wonderland* by Lewis Carroll, *Winnie-the-Pooh* by A. A. Milne, and *Peter and Wendy* by J. M. Barrie. You may also want to check out the more recent prequel to Peter Pan called *Peter and the Starcatchers* by Ridley Pearson and Dave Barry.

FUN ACTIVITIES: Visit the Alice in Wonderland statue in Central Park in New York City, as well as the Winnie-the-Pooh statue at the London Zoo and the Peter Pan statue in Kensington Gardens, both in London

It is not in doing what you like,
but in liking what you do
that is the secret of happiness.

—J. M. Barrie, creator of Peter Pan

PICK AND CELEBRATE A QUOTE THAT INSPIRES YOU

Make a magnet with it to put on your mirror so you see it at the start of each day. Paint the quote on a rock, tile, or piece of cardstock, and glue a magnet to the back of it.

Not feeling crafty? Just use a Post-it note.

(I have included templates of the quotes in this book on bookofdoing.com for you to size, print, color, and laminate.)

SAY THANK YOU...

. . . . to anyone doing something for your benefit or that you benefit from—the sanitation man, the waitress, the hotel maid. Sometimes it is the dirtiest jobs that we take most for granted.

COMPLIMENT THE CHEF

Always thank the person who has prepared your meal. Until you have taken the time to cook a meal for someone, you cannot fully appreciate the effort that goes into it. Find a way to show appreciation for their effort.

SPEND AN HOUR LOOKING AT THE STARS AND LEARNING THE CONSTELLATIONS

DRAW YOUR FAVORITE ONE HERE. ALSO DRAW YOUR BIRTH SIGN CONSTELLATION.

I will never forget looking at the stars above the Jefferson Memorial one night with friends when I was in college. We tend to visit tourist spots during the day, and the combination of this incredible monument all lit up against the star-filled sky was just stunning. We sat for hours trying to find the constellations. I was reminded of this night on a recent trip to Arizona with my family. We saw Saturn through the telescope and it blew us all away. I know when you don't live in a city, you might see this every night, but how often do you take the time to appreciate what is there?

GO TO AN ART MUSEUM AND IMITATE YOUR FAVORITE PIECE ON DISPLAY

So many of us just walk through museums with a bit of a glazed expression, not really engaging or absorbing anything. I once saw a class sitting in front of one picture and drawing it, so I gave it a try. My children and I went to a Georgia O'Keeffe exhibit with pads and colored pencils and each of us picked one of her works to draw. My daughter, Maya, did a beautiful rendition of *Special No. 33.* My son, Max, chose *Tent Door at Night,* a darker piece than the artist is known for, and I attempted *Red and Pink 1925,* which hung among a display of advertising posters Georgia O'Keeffe had done on behalf of a department store early in her career. (I never knew Georgia O'Keeffe had done advertising work!) Max and Maya don't remember the trip to the museum unless I mention our drawings. Experiences are what we remember.

DRAW IT HERE

GIVE THE GIFT OF LAUGHTER

Crowd-source jokes from your friends and *put them together* into a video to share with a friend who can use a laugh. Write the funniest ones here.

When my friend's daughter, Rachel, was going through treatment for an illness, we weren't able to send any physical gifts, but Rachel did have a computer in her room, so my family made a "Gift of Laughter" video and posted it for her to see.

GO ON A PICNIC

It doesn't have to be fancy or homemade. You can even just pick up sandwiches or a pizza. Simply putting your feet in the grass and eating outside is joyous on a beautiful day.

TAKE A NAP
OR SIMPLY GET MORE SLEEP

REM (rapid eye movement) sleep is known to restore your mind, help you process the information you learn each day, and allows your brain to make connections between unrelated information, enabling your creativity to flow. Make a "Do Not Disturb" sign for your door.

Use a hole punch and add ribbon to hang it on your door.

CREATIVE BRAINSTORMING SESSION IN PROGRESS

Please come back later.

TAKE A DIFFERENT ROUTE NEXT TIME YOU GO ON YOUR DAILY WALK OR DRIVE

MAKE YOUR GIFT'S PACKAGING AS SPECIAL AS THE GIFT

Wrap your gifts in brown postal paper and decorate them with drawings, pictures, sponge-paint images, stickers—or whatever will make the recipient smile.

No brown postal paper? Newspaper pages, paper shopping bags, or maps can act as a fun, recycled gift-wrapping canvas, too.

GO TO A FARM. WHERE YOU CAN PICK YOUR OWN FRUITS OR VEGETABLES

MAKE SOMETHING WITH YOUR HARVEST.

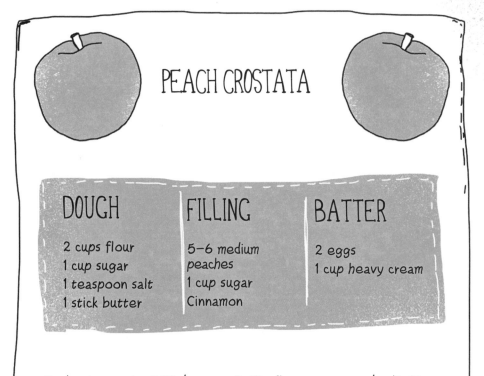

PEACH CROSTATA

DOUGH

2 cups flour
1 cup sugar
1 teaspoon salt
1 stick butter

FILLING

5–6 medium peaches
1 cup sugar
Cinnamon

BATTER

2 eggs
1 cup heavy cream

Preheat oven to 400 degrees F. Mix flour, sugar, and salt. Piece the butter apart with your fingers until mix resembles coarse meal and add to flour mixture.

Press into a 9-inch pie plate. Arrange peaches over the crust and sprinkle with sugar and cinnamon. Bake for 15 minutes.

Meanwhile, beat eggs and cream until blended.

After 15 minutes, remove pie from the oven, pour cream mixture over it, and return it to the oven for 30 minutes.

The crostata can be served warm or at room temperature. It can stay at room temperature for 24 hours, and is best if never refrigerated.

STRAWBERRY JAM

2 pounds fresh strawberries, hulled

4 cups white sugar

1 cup lemon juice

In a wide bowl, crush strawberries in batches until you have 4 cups of mashed berries. In a heavy-bottomed saucepan, mix together the strawberries, sugar, and lemon juice. Stir over low heat until the sugar is dissolved. Increase heat to high and bring the mixture to a rolling boil. Boil, stirring often, until the mixture reaches 220 degrees F.

Transfer to hot sterile jars, leaving 1/4- to 1/2-inch headspace, and seal. Process in a water bath. If the jam is going to be eaten right away, don't bother with processing and just refrigerate.

ISRAELI SALAD

3 cucumbers, peeled and cut in small cubes

3 tomatoes, cut, scooped, and diced into small squares

3 tablespoons chopped fresh parsley

1 lemon, pitted and juiced

2 tablespoons olive oil

Salt to taste

Mix all ingredients together. Chill and serve.

PERFECT YOUR FAVORITE FUNNY FACE

IT WILL COME IN HANDY AT YOUR
NEXT PHOTO SHOOT OR THE NEXT TIME
YOU NEED TO ENTERTAIN A CHILD.
TAKE A PICTURE OF YOURSELF
MAKING THE FACE, AND TAPE IT HERE.

SMELL YOUR DRINK BEFORE TAKING A SIP

...NOT TO MAKE SURE IT'S FRESH, BUT TO APPRECIATE THE AROMA. IT WILL ADD ANOTHER DIMENSION TO YOUR EXPERIENCE.

There are some amazing flavored teas like apple cinnamon or mint that are a combination of aromatherapy and warm soothing liquid. Wines can have a similar effect with the essence of chocolate, berries, citrus, and many other delicious flavors that please the senses and slow you down.

137

PLAY COLOR WAR

Color war is a favorite camp activity that divides campers and counselors into teams to compete in relay races, singing competitions, and just about anything else you can imagine. It is extremely fun and gets competitive juices flowing. But there's no need to go to summer camp to play color war. Get a group together, divide into two teams, and spend a day doing relay races and camp activities. It's great to inspire bonding of all kinds—families, friends, teams. Plus it produces lots of laughter. Some games include running relays, egg on a spoon or egg toss, three-legged races, potato sack races, and bucket brigade.

My sister, Cindy, turned color war into a family activity a few years ago to celebrate our dad's sixty-fifth birthday. Now, every year, we have three generations playing together, laughing together, and getting pretty competitive and silly. Every family is dysfunctional in some way, but this is a great way to get everyone together and focusing only on the fun on the agenda.

WHO WILL BE ON EACH TEAM?

WHAT WILL YOUR TEAM NAMES BE?

WHAT ACTIVITIES WILL YOU PLAY?

WHAT SUPPLIES WILL YOU NEED?

LOOK AT THE WORLD THROUGH A CAMERA LENS

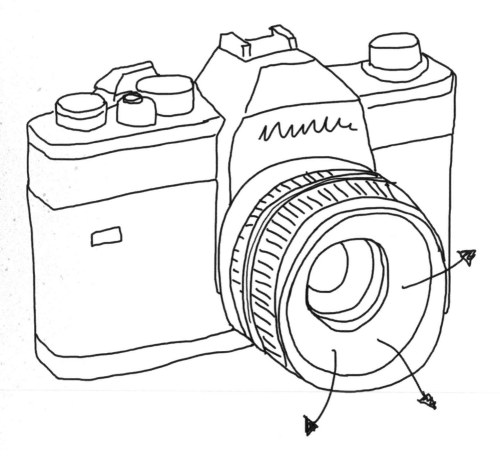

A camera will help you zoom in on the beautiful and interesting things around you and see things from new angles. Over time, this enables you to capture moments in your mind, appreciate the changing light, and notice incredible details you may not have focused on previously.

BECOME A MOBILE PHOTOGRAPHER TOO

Snap and send *pictures of things you see that remind you of others*. If it makes you smile, chances are it will *have the same effect on them*.

I once chose international calling and mobile *photography* over good local calling from a carrier I knew didn't have strong coverage in New York. I dropped calls all over Manhattan, but, boy, did I send some great mobile pictures from overseas at times when I felt really far away from loved ones. While not for everyone, it was a perfect decision for me at the time.

IN BUSINESS AND IN LIFE IT IS OFTEN ESSENTIAL TO LOOK AT THINGS FROM A COMPLETELY DIFFERENT ANGLE.

SWEAT

It doesn't have to be every day and it doesn't have to be for long, but find time to do it a few times each week. There are lots of ways to sweat—either with friends or alone. Run, dance, turn on the music really loud while you're cleaning the house—just sweat while you're doing it. It is not just about the exercise. It's a release that will de-stress you and free your brain.

CREATE YOUR OWN HOLIDAY CARDS, BIRTHDAY CARDS, OR THANK-YOU NOTES

USE THEM WHENEVER YOU GIVE A GIFT OR SIMPLY TO SHOW APPRECIATION. BE SURE TO SIGN THE BACK SO THE RECIPIENT KNOWS IT WAS MADE BY YOU.

SIGNING YOUR WORK IS THE FIRST STEP IN TAKING OWNERSHIP FOR YOUR IDEAS AND CREATIONS. DON'T BE SHY ABOUT IT.

KNOW YOUR FLOWERS

NAME THEM. COLOR THEM. PAINT BY NUMBERS.

- PEONY — Healing
- ORCHID — Delicate beauty
- DAISY — Innocence
- IRIS (purple) — Wisdom
- ROSE — Love (plus many other things depending on the color)
- DAHLIA — Good taste
- HYDRANGEA — Friendship

THE MEANINGS BEHIND ROSE COLORS:

RED — Love, respect, courage, congratulations
PINK — Happiness, romance, admiration, sweetness
YELLOW — Welcome back, friendship, caring, joy
WHITE — Innocence, purity, secrecy, reverence
LAVENDER/PURPLE — Deep adoration, majestic, opulent
PEACH — Gratitude, appreciation, sincerity, modesty
ORANGE/CORAL — Desire, enthusiasm, pride
BLACK/DEEP RED — New beginnings and rebirth

TIP: Always cut flowers at the base of the stem on a diagonal with a sharp knife or scissors, so they can absorb the most water.

FUN FACT: A little bit of vodka, soda, or bleach can be added to water to keep flowers alive longer.

MEDITATE FOR A FEW MINUTES EACH DAY

Close your eyes and pay attention to your breath. Visualize breathing white light in and black air out. Set an intention for your meditation time that focuses you on the act of meditation. Your intention may be simply to stay in the moment and relax, or to let go of anger or stress that is clouding your day. Setting a purpose will help center you and clear your mind.

The first time I attempted meditation was in a yoga class with my husband. I giggled the whole time. I just didn't get it. I tried again when I had a foot injury and couldn't run for a while. I now crave and appreciate the importance of meditation in centering myself and my day. It doesn't need to be in a yoga class, just a few minutes with your eyes closed in a quiet place will work. No time to meditate? Just remember to breathe. It's amazing how often we forget.

ANCIENT LEGEND: If you sit in a forward bend position for 24 hours straight it will bring you eternal joy. Perhaps 15 minutes a day in this position may add a bit of happiness to your day.

CREATE A "MY FAVORITE THINGS" BOX

USE IT TO COLLECT YOUR FAVORITE MEMENTOS. WHAT SHOULD GO IN IT?

Do one thing every day that scares you.

—Eleanor Roosevelt

DO SOMETHING THAT SCARES YOU

Eleanor Roosevelt said it, but stepping out of your comfort zone can be mind-expanding and liberating. "Scary" is a matter of perspective and different for everyone. For me, the scariest thing I needed to overcome was speaking on stage. There were many other things I needed to overcome along the way, some of which I have wiped from memory, as the more you do them, the less scary things become. Whether speaking to someone you've been avoiding or jumping out of an airplane . . . whatever it is for you—go do it.

LEARN TO PLAY CHESS

I play with my son, Max, and he usually proudly kicks my butt, but it gives us quiet time together with a game all about strategy.

What Do the Different Pieces Do?

KING
Moves one square in any direction

QUEEN
Moves as many squares as desired in any single direction

ROOK
Moves any number of squares horizontally or vertically

BISHOP
Moves any number of squares diagonally

KNIGHT
Moves two squares forward and one square to the side

PAWN
Moves two squares horizontally from its starting point and one square horizontally on all subsequent moves

MAKE YOUR OWN CHESSBOARD

1. Start with square wood (approximately 8 1/2 x 8 1/2 inches).

2. Measure a 1/4-inch border around perimeter.

3. Measure 64 squares.

4. Paint it white or whatever base color you choose.

5. When dry, use tape to cover alternating squares.

6. Paint it black or any color other than the base color.

7. Paint the border.

Theme Ideas for Pieces: Salt and pepper shakers (glass or ceramic), favorite childhood figurines, whatever else you can dream up

What else could you make with a plain wooden board?

MAKE UP A NEW CAR GAME

My family took punch-buggy to another level. Every time we see a Mini Cooper we call out "Mini red and white" or whatever color it is, making the Mini face at the same time. Here's how to make the Mini face: Put your hand up to your chin as if you're imitating a begging puppy, and make doe eyes as you do it.

MY CAR GAME:

_____
_____
_____
_____
_____
_____
_____
_____
_____
_____
_____
_____

FIX SOMETHING

Sometimes we don't think we have the capability to fix something. Then we try to fix it—whether it's a friendship that was broken long ago, or a bedside lamp. When we succeed, we wonder why we waited so long in the first place. Give it a try. It will be worth the effort.

My husband recently mended his busted baseball glove with a kit he found at a sporting goods store. Who knew he didn't have to buy a whole new one?! He was so proud of himself that he posted pictures of the activity on Facebook.

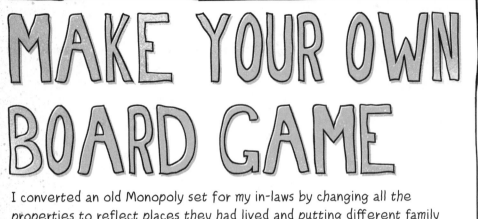

MAKE YOUR OWN BOARD GAME

I converted an old Monopoly set for my in-laws by changing all the properties to reflect places they had lived and putting different family members' faces on the money. It was a sweet gift, but it also encouraged my in-laws to share new stories about all the places they had lived.

GET OVER IT

Don't wait until something really bad happens to realize how good things are. Make amends, celebrate, get perspective, and identify what's causing you unhappiness or holding you back from doing the things you want so you can just let it go. We all have something that falls into this category. What is it for you?

1.

2.

3.

Make a list of five people you love and five things you love to do.
Make sure they figure prominently into your schedule.

PEOPLE I LOVE

1 _____

2 _____

3 _____

4 _____

5 _____

THINGS I LOVE TO DO

1 _____

2 _____

3 _____

4 _____

5 _____

WRITE A BOOK

Everyone has at least one in them. What will yours be about?
Write your topics here. Now take a stab at the chapter outline.

MAKE EVERY MINUTE COUNT

IF I HAD LIMITED TIME ON THE PLANET, I WOULD:

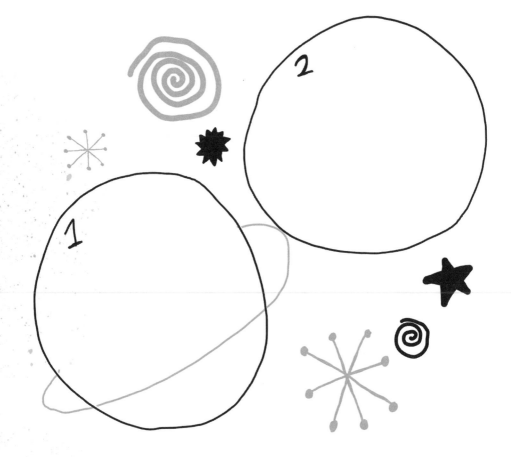

Guess what? You do have limited time on the planet, so what's stopping you? Go do it!

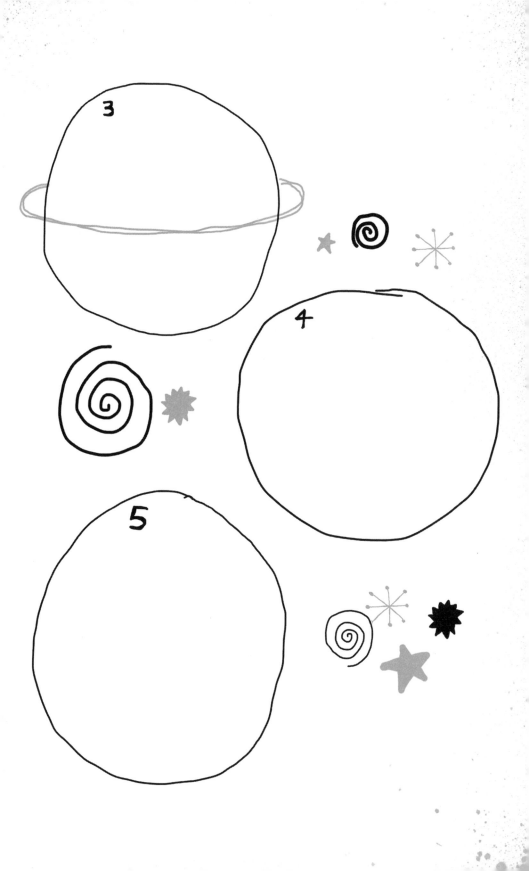

Don't you ever let a soul
in the world tell you
that you can't be
exactly who you are.

—Lady Gaga

WHAT DO YOU WANT TO DO?

Projects can be big or small, but life is a project that becomes better when you apply your creativity to it. Following are some calendars and project pages to help you track your ideas and action steps, and help you in your doing. Don't be concerned if you only know the first few steps before you set out. The rest will become clear as you do.

One of the biggest excuses people give for not doing the things they love is lack of time. Track your days to see where you might be able to make different choices to find some hidden moments.

	Sunday	Monday	Tuesday
Morning			
Afternoon			
Evening			

Wednesday	Thursday	Friday	Saturday

DAYS OF

Track all the new ways you are adding doing to your days.

Month: _____

DAYS OF

Track all the new ways you are adding doing to your days.

Month: _____

MY PROJECT:

VISION:

WHO CAN HELP:

WHAT DO I NEED?:

STEP 1:

STEP 2:

STEP 3:

MY PROJECT:

VISION:

WHO CAN HELP:

WHAT DO I NEED?:

STEP 1:

STEP 2:

STEP 3:

MY PROJECT:

VISION:

WHO CAN HELP:

WHAT DO I NEED?:

STEP 1:

STEP 2:

STEP 3:

MY PROJECT:

VISION:

WHO CAN HELP:

WHAT DO I NEED?:

STEP 1:

STEP 2:

STEP 3:

MY PROJECT:

VISION:

WHO CAN HELP:

WHAT DO I NEED?:

STEP 1:

STEP 2:

STEP 3:

VISION:

WHO CAN HELP:

WHAT DO I NEED?:

STEP 1:

STEP 2:

STEP 3:

MY PROJECT:

VISION:

WHO CAN HELP:

WHAT DO I NEED?:

STEP 1:

STEP 2:

STEP 3:

MY PROJECT:

VISION:

WHO CAN HELP:

WHAT DO I NEED?:

STEP 1:

STEP 2:

STEP 3:

MY PROJECT:

VISION:

WHO CAN HELP:

WHAT DO I NEED?:

STEP 1:

STEP 2:

STEP 3:

MY PROJECT:

VISION:

WHO CAN HELP:

WHAT DO I NEED?:

STEP 1:

STEP 2:

STEP 3:

WANT TO HELP WITH THE NEXT BOOK OF DOING?

Help me create a movement, and write the next edition.
Go to bookofdoing.com and share an activity you do to help drive creativity.

ACKNOWLEDGMENTS

My first thank-you goes to my very first arts-and-crafts teacher, Frieda Rubin, who inspired me with feathers, Popsicle sticks, googly eyes, and paints in a little shack in the Catskill Mountains when I was five years old. Realizing my personal ability to create something delightful from nothing is a life lesson for which I will always be grateful.

The beauty of exploration is that it leads you to new people and places, and also sometimes back to amazing relationships you haven't connected with in a while. Mine thankfully led me to both. On the new side, a huge thank-you to my agent, Wayne Kabak, for embracing my first book and an arts-and-crafts kid. To my editor, Meg Leder, for allowing me to fail forward and for being open to another possibility so we could create The Book of Doing together. To Adam James Turnbull, the brilliant illustrator who responded to a message in a bottle email from the other side of the world with the enthusiasm and understanding that fill every page of this book. You're amazing. My writing has also led me back to two of my first friends, Brad Meltzer and Erica Klein, both students of Frieda Rubin. I could never have imagined then the amazing ways we could work together now. Our conversations throughout this project have been some of my favorite of the past two years.

I am extraordinarily thankful for an amazing support system. My mom and dad, Sharon and Julian Price, and my sister and brother, Cindy and Craig, have been with me as I learned so many of the lessons that shape this book. My mother- and father-in-law, Verna and Irwin, sisters- and brothers-in-law, and nieces and nephews have been such a happy part of so many of the activities and stories I have shared. A special thank-you to my Ad Age family for incredible support and encouragement: Rance Crain, Gloria Scoby, David Klein, Angela Carola, Jackie Ghedine, Meilyn Castillo, and the rest of our team. I love the opportunities and challenges that come with creating the future of such an iconic brand.

Then there are the amazing angels who help, encourage, and inspire you along the way; I have had too many to name. A special thank-you to Michelle Simmons, Anne Bologna, Tom Repicci, James Gregorio, Brett Jaffe, Jill Drossman, Claire Goodhue, Scott Lowry, and Jill Rothman. And, of course, the ladies of the Martini Project—a special crew that helped me appreciate the importance of sharing some of your absurdity with others.

And finally, to Max, Maya, and Scott. Thank you for being mine, making every day an adventure, and for your never-ending sense of humor. Yes, Maya, I know . . . you got it from your dad. xoxo

ABOUT THE AUTHOR

Allison Arden has translated her childhood love of arts and crafts into a lean-forward life philosophy, helping transform personal perspective to have a positive impact on business and life.

As a full-time working married mom of two young children, Allison has learned that the only way to make it all work together is to approach every activity and every day with joy and wonder, a sense of humor, and a "never say die" willingness to figure it out and get your hands dirty. We, and everything around us, are an ongoing work in progress.

In addition, Allison is publisher of *Advertising Age*, leading the transformation of an eighty-year-old iconic media brand serving a market upended by change. While business continues to evolve, Allison believes that everything is still about people and our ability to lean into change and the opportunities that come with it that make the difference between success and failure.

Born and bred in Brooklyn, Allison now lives in Manhattan with her husband, Scott, their two children, Max, 10, and Maya, 7, and their chocolate lab, Rosie. It is through her children that Allison has rediscovered her love for arts and crafts. Follow Allison on Twitter @allisonarden.

Find *The Book of Doing* online: boofofdoing.com

or

Join the conversation on Twitter: #bookofdoing

ABOUT THE ILLUSTRATOR

As a child Adam James Turnbull (as he is affectionately known to his closest friends and family) always dreamed of being a businessman, a man who would wear mediocre suits, drive a mediocre car, and be heavily involved in "business."

Fortunately Adam's corporate dreams were smashed to smithereens at the age of eight when he discovered crayons on the table of a well-known chain of family restaurants.

Never looking back, Adam has pursued his secondary dream and is surprisingly quite good at it.

Adam has been drawing and illustrating professionally since finding those crayons; however, it was eight years ago that he studied and started working with clients.

His illustrations have been seen all over the world in some very famous and some very not-famous publications, all of which Adam is very proud. His mother also assures him she is proud every chance she gets.

Adam currently resides and works in Sydney, Australia, and is represented by a myriad of colorful button-up shirts, a pair of glasses, and his agent Colagene (USA, Canada, Europe & UK).